THE MUSICIANS LIBRARY
NINETY-FIVE VOLUMES ISSUED

* All song volumes are issued for both High and Low Voice, except where otherwise stated.

FIFTY SHAKSPERE SONGS

FIFTY
SHAKSPERE SONGS

EDITED BY
CHARLES VINCENT
(MUS. DOC. OXON.)

FOR HIGH VOICE

THE
MUSICIANS
LIBRARY

Boston : **OLIVER DITSON COMPANY** : New York

Chicago : **LYON & HEALY, Inc.** London : **WINTHROP ROGERS, Ltd.**

MUSIC TO SHAKSPERE'S SONGS

FEW subjects could present greater attractions to a student of English song than a survey of the music composed to the verses written by the greatest of bards, William Shakspere,[1] embracing as it does a period from the end of the sixteenth century to the present time. Almost every musician of ability since Shakspere's time has set some of his verses; therefore a collection of this music, arranged in chronological order, must illustrate in a very practical manner the growth of style, the improvements in harmonic combinations, the freedom introduced into melodic passages, and the gradual development which has taken place in music generally, from the time when it was yet in its infancy to the present advanced state of the art.

It is desirable in as few words as possible to show the condition of England, historically as well as musically, at the time when the poet was producing and performing his plays. Then Queen Elizabeth was on the throne, and her long and memorable reign was nearing its close (she died in 1603). Owing to the introduction of the printing-press, that great lever to education, a desire for knowledge of every kind had sprung up among the more cultured classes of the people. English ships, commanded by such adventurous and gallant sailors as Drake and Hawkins, were adding to our possessions over the seas, and opening up new outlets for ambition and fame. Patriotism had been greatly stimulated by the scattering of that great fleet sent by Spain to conquer the little island. The reformation of religion had been accomplished; and the results—freedom of thought and more liberal education—were aiding in the general development. This active epoch brought to the front great leaders in science, theology, politics and art, among the latter the great immortal dramatist and poet, Shakspere, whose genius has set down for all time the thoughts and emotions of this wonderful and stirring period.

The condition of English music also reflected the brilliance of the times, as has been well stated by Hullah in the following passage: "In the sixteenth century we not only sang and played as much and as well as our neighbours, but we sang and played our own music. It is no exaggeration to say that the English hold, and are recognized as holding, a very high place among the composers of the period. Tallis, Farrant, Byrd and Bevin, in 'the service high and anthem clear;' Morley, Ward, Wilbye and Weelkes in the madrigal; Bull, in performance as well as in composition; Dowland, 'the friend of Shakspere,' in the part song; and, last and greatest in all styles, Orlando Gibbons—these are all names to which the English musician may refer with confidence and with pride, as fit to be associated with those of Palestrina, De Lattre and Marenzio. . . . Our insular position, which has favoured us in so many things, has favoured us in the individuality of our music, and left our composers of earlier times more to their own resources than those of any other country. Indeed, a comparison of dates shows us to be rather the precursors than the followers of other nations." During the Elizabethan reign, the madrigalian period attained its highest development, and though it was not the music of the people, so to speak, it showed the refinement, activity, ingenuity and taste of a race of musicians, the outcome of the period, who proved their ability to compete successfully with the best of other nations.

---

[1] *This spelling of the great poet's name is taken from the only unquestionably genuine signatures of his that we possess, the three on his will, and the two on his Blackfriars conveyance and mortgage. None of these signatures have an e after the k; four have no a after the first e; the fifth has the overline open-topt a (or u) which is the usual contraction for ra, but must here have been meant for re. The a and e had their French sounds, which explain the forms "Shaxper," &c. (New Shakspere Society Proceedings.)*

It is probable that Shakspere wrote some of the songs in his plays to music which was already in existence and popular at the time, as many poets have done since, notably Burns and Thomas Moore. A search by the editor on these lines, however, has not been fruitful. Unless some important evidence is forthcoming, from one place or another, it is unlikely that we can ever arrive at a definite conclusion; for with the destruction of the Globe Theatre by fire in 1613 most of the performing MSS., including the music, were burnt. This disastrous circumstance, however, adds zest to the student's research, and we may yet hope to recover some of the clues which, if carefully followed, will lead to much more interesting knowledge on the subject than we at present possess.

Only in a very few cases can we feel certain that we possess the exact music that was performed in the plays during Shakspere's time. These songs are given in Part II, though exception may be taken to No. 14, "Take, O take those lips away." To the songs included in Part II might be added the airs sung by Ophelia (*Hamlet*), to be found in Chappell's *Musical Magazine*, No. 47, and in other collections; for they are generally considered to be the originals.

With regard to No. 14, if it be the original musical setting of the words, it is improbable that John Wilson composed it : he might have been the boy who sang it,—probably he was,—in which case the music might have been by Robert Johnson, or some other theatre musician. Dr. John Wilson has been identified with the "Jackie Wilson" who sang in the plays. (See note to No. 13.)

One good ground for the supposition that "Jackie Wilson" is one with Dr. John Wilson, vocalist and composer, is the fact that at a later date (1653) John Wilson published in his book entitled *Select Ayres* the song "Take, O take those lips away," and in 1660, in *Cheerful Ayres and Ballads first Composed for One Single Voice and since Set for Three Voices* he included the following songs by Shakspere, with which Jackie Wilson would have become familiar during his connec-

tion with the theatre: "From the fair Lavinian Shore;" "Full fathom five" (R. Johnson); "Where the bee sucks" (R. Johnson); "When love with unconfined wings," and "Lawn as white as driven snow" (R. Johnson?). These songs Wilson must have had a special liking for, otherwise he would not have included them in his books, and had he not done so, in all probability they would have been lost.

An examination of the music performed in the plays in Shakspere's time shows us that it must have been simple and melodious, rather than difficult and contrapuntal; an additional reason in support of this view being, that in all probability the actors themselves would sing the songs, and boys, with treble voices, always performed the female parts.

Even if we have any doubt as to the character of the music performed in the plays, we can have none as to what the music of the period was like, at least that portion of it which was well known to Shakspere; for he has referred to a considerable number of songs, &c., in the several plays, many of which the editor has been able to examine, and no doubt more can be found if diligent search be made. These are all of the simple and melodious character, and as so few are accessible to the public, or even published at all in modern collections, seven have been selected, from a large number, and printed as Part I of this collection. It is thought that they will not only prove interesting, but historically valuable to all lovers of music, and more especially to students of the songs of our ancestors. An additional reason for including these songs is that they give the reader a good idea of the class of music in vogue at the time the plays were written, and enable him to trace the developments which follow.

To make anything like a complete collection of the music which has been written to Shakspere's verses would be impossible; attention has therefore been chiefly confined to songs which occur in the plays.

There are some examples of Shakspere's verses set to music during his lifetime which are now obtainable; they are not, however, of the kind required for this volume. Among such may be mentioned three madrigals by Weelkes set to verses out of *The Passionate Pilgrim:* "In black mourn I," "My flocks feed not" and "Clear wells spring not."

When we examine the music written for performances of the plays at a period soon after the death of Shakspere, of which we have plenty of data, we find it to be of a natural, melodious character. As this would be composed somewhat on the lines of that which had previously been successfully employed, we may with reason conclude that it was the folk style of music (rather than the involved contrapuntal) which was heard in the original representations of the plays. This subject has been dwelt on rather fully, as there is an idea that, owing to the then popularity of the madrigal, the madrigal style (contrapuntal) might have been employed in the early performances.

The accompaniments were played by the musicians who were placed in the upper gallery, situated above what we now call the stage box. The band consisted of about eight or ten performers on hautboys, lutes, recorders (flageolets), cornets (not the modern cornet), viols and organs (a kind of small portable organ). The band announced the beginning of the play by three "soundings" or flourishes; they also played between the acts. Incidental music was required of them, likewise soft music through which speaking could be heard, called "still music."

As most of the examples in Parts I and II and some few in Part III exist only as melodies, or with very crude accompaniments, the editor has added a pianoforte part in order that the work may be practical and useful and not merely an antiquarian collection. At the same time he has endeavored to make these accompaniments somewhat characteristic of the period to which the melodies belong.

The collection is divided into four parts:

Part I. Songs mentioned by Shakspere in the Plays.

Part II. Songs possibly sung in the Original Performances.

Part III. Settings composed since Shakspere's time to the middle of the Nineteenth Century.

Part IV. Recent Settings.

The editor desires to express his indebtedness and thanks to Mr. J. Greenhill for so kindly permitting him to examine and make use of his extensive collection of Shakspere music. Mr. Greenhill was the musical director of the New Shakspere Society (now disbanded), and, together with the Rev. W. A. Harrison and Mr. F. J. Furnivall, compiled *All the Songs and Passages in Shakspere which have been set to Music* (Thübner).

Charles Vincent

The Coppice
Pinner, November 5, 1905.

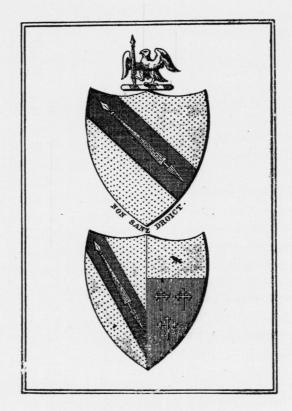

THE ARMS OF SHAKSPERE

NOTES ON THE SONGS
PART I. SONGS MENTIONED BY SHAKSPERE IN HIS PLAYS

No. 1. *Farewell, dear love.*

THIS song is quoted line by line in *Twelfth Night*, Act II, scene iii, by Sir Toby Belch:

Malvolio. An' it would please you to take leave of her, she is very willing to bid you farewell.

Toby. "Farewell, dear heart, for I must needs be gone."

Maria. Nay, good Sir Toby.

Clown. "His eyes do show his days are almost done."

Mal. Is 't even so?

Toby. "But I will never die."

Clo. Sir Toby, there you lie.

Mal. This is much credit to you.

Toby. "Shall I bid him go and spare not?"

Clo. "Oh, no, no, no, no, you dare not."

The lines quoted are adapted by Shakspere from the first verse of the old ballad "Corydon's Farewell to Phillis," printed in 1590.

The music was composed by Robert Jones, the lutenist, and is found in Book I of his *Songs and Ayres set out for the Lute*, published in 1601. The date of Robert Jones' birth is unknown, but he graduated at Oxford, taking his Mus. Bac. degree in 1597. Many of his compositions exist in published works of the period; he was also a contributor to *The Triumphs of Oriana*. The song "Farewell, dear love" was at a later date introduced into *As You Like It*.

No. 2. *Peg o' Ramsay.*

MENTION is also made of this ballad in *Twelfth Night*, Act II, scene iii. Sir Toby Belch says:

My lady's a Cataian, we are politicians, Malvolio's a "Peg o' Ramsay" and "Three merry men be we."

The verses "Bonny Peggie Ramsay" occur in *Wit and Mirth*, 1719, and in all probability they are the words of the ballad alluded to in the play. They exactly fit the old tune of that name.

The tune is found in a manuscript book by Dr. Bull, from the late Dr. Kitchiner's library, and is very quaint. The subdominant chord connecting the parts (see measure 8, &c.) gives the effect of a kind of round, the parts following in an almost interminable way. It is the editor's idea that this song (and others of a similar character) was sung when several country folk gathered together, the burden being repeated over and over again, one of the singers jumping in, so to speak, with a strong lead, "with a hey tro-lo-del," almost before the previous refrain was finished. He has often heard such songs in remote country districts sung in this way. After the refrain "with a hey" has been repeated four or five times, a chance is given to the soloist to give another verse; and so on to the end of the ballad.

No. 3. *Green-Sleeves.*

SHAKSPERE mentions this tune twice in the *Merry Wives*. In Act II, scene i, Mrs. Ford, in speaking of Falstaff to Mrs. Page, says: "I would have sworn his disposition would have gone to the truth of his words; but they do no more adhere and keep pace than the Hundredth Psalm to the tune of 'Green-Sleeves.'" This is an interesting quotation, showing that Shakspere could think of no more rollicking tune to contrast with the solemnity of the Hundredth Psalm.

The second mention of the tune is in Act V, scene v, where Falstaff says:

Let the sky rain potatoes;
Let it thunder to the tune of "Green-sleeves."

The tune is found in W. Ballet's *Lute Book*, and doubtless was very popular at the time the play was written; though Chappell shows that it must have been a tune of Henry VIII's reign. The earliest mention of the ballad is to be found in the *Stationers' Register* for September, 1580; the ballad is much older than this, however, and runs as follows:

A new Courtly Sonet, of the Lady Greensleeues. To the new tune of Greensleeues.

> Greensleeues was all my ioy,
> Greensleeues was my delight:
> Greensleeues was my hart of gold:
> And who but Ladie Greensleeues?

ALAS my loue, ye do me wrong, to caste me off discurteously:

And I haue louĕd you so long,
    Delighting in your companie.
        Greensleeues was all my ioy,
          Greensleeues was my delight:
        Greensleeues was my heart of gold;
          And who but Ladie Greensleeues?

I haue been readie at your hand,
    to grant what euer you would craue.
I haue both waged life and land,
    your loue and good will for to haue.
        Greensleeues was all my ioy, &c.

I bought thee kerchers to thy head,
    that were wrought fine and gallantly:
I kept thee both at boord and bed,
    Which cost my purse wel fauouredly:
        Greensleeues was al my ioie, &c.

I bought thee peticotes of the best,
    the cloth so fine as fine might be:
I gaue thee iewels for thy chest,
    and all this cost I spent on thee.
        Greensleeues was all my ioie, &c.

Thy smock of silk, both faire and white,
    with gold embrodered gorgeously:
Thy peticote of Sendall right:
    and thus I bought thee gladly.
        Greensleeues was all my ioie, &c.

Thy girdle [1] of gold so red,
    with pearles bedecked sumptuously:
The like no other lasses had,
    and yet thou wouldst not loue me!
        Greensleeues was all my ioy, &c.

Thy purse and eke thy gay guilt kniues,
    thy pincase gallant to the eie:
No better wore the Burgesse wiues;
    and yet thou wouldst not loue me!
        Greensleeues was all my ioy, &c.

Thy crimson stockings all of silk,
    with golde all wrought aboue the knee;
Thy pumps as white as was the milk;
    and yet thou wouldst not loue me!
        Greensleeues was all my ioy, &c.

Thy gown was of the grassie [2] green,
    thy sleeues of Satten hanging by:

Which made thee be our haruest Queen,
    and yet thou wouldst not loue me!
        Greensleeues was all my ioy, &c.

Thy garters fringĕd with the golde,
    And siluer aglets hanging by,
Which made thee blithe for to beholde:
    And yet thou wouldst not loue me!
        Greensleeues was all my ioy, &c.

My gayest gelding I thee gaue,
    To ride where euer likĕd thee;
No Ladie euer was so braue;
    And yet thou wouldst not loue me!
        Greensleeues was all my ioy, &c.

My men were clothed all in green,
    And they did euer wait on thee:
Al this was gallant to be seen;
    and yet thou wouldst not loue me!
        Greensleeues was all my ioy, &c.

They set thee vp, they took thee downe,
    they serued thee with humilitie;
Thy foote might not once touch the ground;
    and yet thou wouldst not loue me!
        Greensleeues was all my ioy, &c.

For euerie morning when thou rose,
    I sent thee dainties orderly,
To cheare thy stomack from all woes;
    and yet thou wouldst not loue me!
        Greensleeues was all my ioy, &c.

Thou couldst desire no earthly thing,
    But stil thou hadst it readily:
Thy musicke still to play and sing:
    And yet thou wouldst not loue me!
        Greensleeues was all my ioy, &c.

And who did pay for all this geare,
    that thou didst spend when pleased thee?
Euen I that am reieḷed here;
    and thou disdainst to loue me.
        Greensleeues was all my ioy, &c.

Wel, I wil pray to God on hie,
    that thou my constancie maist see:
And that yet once before I die,
    thou wilt vouchsafe to loue me.
        Greensleeues was all my ioy, &c.

[1] Girdle *is either three syllables, or an adjective like "fine" is left out after it.*
[2] Grossie *in original.*

Greensleeues, now farewel, adue!
  God I pray, to prosper thee:
For I am stil thy louer true:
  Come once againe, and loue me!
    Greensleeues was all my ioy, &c.

No. 4. *Heigh-ho! for a husband.*

THIS song is twice mentioned in *Much Ado About Nothing*, Act II, scene i:

Beatrice. Thus goes every one to the world but I, and I am sunburnt. I may sit in a corner and cry "heigh-ho for a husband!"

Act III, scene iv:

Beatrice. By my troth, I am exceeding ill; heigh-ho!
Margaret. For a hawk, a horse, or a husband?
Beatrice. For the letter that begins them all, H.

"Heigh-ho! for a husband" is an old ballad in The Pepysian Collection. Chappell says it is to be found in *A Complete Collection of Old and New English and Scotch Songs with New Tunes Prefixed*. It also occurs in *Wit and Mirth* (1719), from which it is given with a few slight alterations, made by the Rev. W. A. Harrison for performance at one of the meetings of the New Shakspere Society in 1887.

The tune is taken from John Gamble's manuscript *Common-place Book*. John Gamble died in 1657. The accompaniment is specially arranged for this collection by the editor.

No. 5. *Heart's Ease.*

THIS tune is mentioned in *Romeo and Juliet*, Act IV, scene v:

Peter. Musicians, O musicians, "Heart's ease, Heart's ease." Oh! an you will have me live, play "Heart's ease."
First Musician. Why "Heart's ease"?
Peter. O musicians, because my heart itself plays, "My heart is full of woe." Oh! play me some merry dump, to comfort me.

The tune is an old one, much older than the words, for in an old play, *Misogonus*, by Thomas Rychardes, produced about 1560 (the manuscript is dated 1577), in the second act occurs the song, with directions that it "be sung to the tune of 'Heart's Ease.'"

The tune is in a manuscript volume of lute music of the sixteenth century in the Public Library, Cambridge, D. d. ii 11.

No. 6. *Light o' Love.*

IT is not absolutely certain that the verses are from the original song. They are by Leonard Gybson, and were first printed in 1570, in Stuth's *Ancient Ballads and Broadsides*. There are thirteen verses in all, but only the first two are given, being perhaps sufficient for the purpose of illustration.

The tune is twice alluded to by Shakspere; in *The Two Gentlemen of Verona*, Act I, scene ii:

Julia. Some love of yours, hath writ to you in rhyme.
Lucetta. That I might sing it, madam, to a tune. Give me a note: your ladyship can set.
Julia. As little by such toys as may be possible. Best sing it to the tune of "Light o' love."

Much Ado About Nothing, Act III, scene iv:

Beat. I am out of all other tune, methinks.
Mar. Clap us into "Light o' love;" that goes without a burden: do you sing it, and I'll dance it.
Beat. Ye light o' love with your heels, &c.

In the preface to the *Shakspere Album or Warwickshire Garland*, "Light o' love" is spoken of as Shakspere's favorite tune.

The editor has felt obliged to make some little variation in the accompaniment on account of the frequent repetitions of the same phrase.

No. 7. *Three merry men be we.*

THIS song is mentioned in *Twelfth Night* by Sir Toby Belch in the same paragraph as that in which "Peg o' Ramsay" is referred to, Act II, scene iii.

In the tragedy of *Rollo, Duke of Normandy*, by John Fletcher, the song is expanded as given in No. 7, except for the omission of the second verse, which is left out in order to render the song consistent with the refrain, for in *Rollo* the ballad is for four persons to sing.

The song appears to be a grumble by certain men condemned to be hanged, who in the refrain endeavor to keep up their spirits by singing in a jovial though sarcastic manner the words "Three merry men be we."

This song was arranged by Mr. Greenhill in an ingenious way for one of the meetings of the New Shakspere Society, and he has kindly allowed use to be made of his manuscript. The editor has availed himself of this permission to a considerable extent, as far as the airs are concerned.

Verse I is set to "Fortune my Foe," found in *Queen Elizabeth's Virginal Book*, also in W. Ballet's manuscript *Lute Book*. It is mentioned in *The Merry Wives*, Act III, scene iii, and was sometimes called "The Hanging Tune." Chappell is of opinion that this is the original tune for the first verse; and indeed such conclusion appears to be most probable. *The Refrain* after each verse is from a manuscript *Common-place Book* in the handwriting of John Playford. *Verse II* consists of two very old tunes, "The Jolly Pinder" and "The Friar and the Nun." *Verse III* is set to the well-known tune "Watkins' Ale" as arranged by Byrd in *Queen Elizabeth's Virginal Book*.

This fine tune must have been well known at the period; the refrain has certainly done duty many times since, in one form or another.

The editor is not aware of any complete list of the songs to which Shakspere refers in the plays. In addition to the seven given here he has collected the following: "King Cophetua;" "The Sick Tune;" "When Arthur first;" "Come o'er the bourne, Bessie;" "Death, rock me to sleep;" "Hold thy peace, thou knave;" "There dwelt a man in Babylon, lady, lady;" "Oh, the twelfth day of December;" "Jog on;" "Whop! do me no harm, good man;" "I loathe that I did love" (three stanzas from which are sung by the grave-digger in *Hamlet*); "Dildos and fadings," and "Can you not hit it, my good man."

For information about the various English composers of early times, *British Musical Biography*, by Brown & Stratton, is the most concise and reliable.

PART II. SONGS POSSIBLY SUNG IN THE ORIGINAL PERFORMANCES

THESE songs were performed during Shakspere's lifetime, and probably under his direction.

No. 8. *The Willow Song.*
From OTHELLO, *Act IV, scene iii.*
THE music of this song is exceedingly old. It is to be found in Thomas Dallis's manuscript *Lute-Book* under the title "All a green willow." The book is dated 1583, and is now in the library of Trinity College, Dublin. A version of the song is also to be found in the British Museum.

Shakspere adapted the words from the old song to suit Desdemona, who sings it while her maid Æmilia is undressing her to go to the bed in which Othello strangles her.

There can be no doubt that this song was sung under Shakspere's direction, and is most interesting on that account. Apart from this connection the song itself is beautiful and full of character and feeling.

No. 9. *O Mistress Mine.*
From TWELFTH NIGHT, *Act II, scene iii.*
THE melody of this song is anonymous. Two versions exist,—one arranged by Morley in the first book of *Consort Lessons*, 1599; the other arranged by Byrd in *Queen Elizabeth's Virginal Book*, 1611. The second version of the melody has been selected, as it appears to be the better of the two. It is harmonized by the editor.

The song is introduced as follows:

Sir Andrew. Excellent! Why, this is the best fooling, when all is done. Now, a song.

Sir Toby. Come on; there is sixpence for you: let's have a song.

Sir Andrew. There's a testril of me too: if one knight give a—

Clown. Would you have a love-song, or a song of good life?

Sir Toby. A love-song, a love-song.

Sir Andrew. Ay, ay: I care not for good life.

Clown sings, "O mistress mine."

At the end of the first verse Sir Andrew says, "Excellent good i' faith," and Sir Toby adds, "Good, good." Then the Clown sings the second verse.

No. 10. *It was a lover and his lass.*
From As You Like It, *Act V, scene iii.*
THIS song, or rather duet,—for it should be sung by two pages in the play,—was composed by Thomas Morley, and is published, as given here,

in the first book of *Ayres or Little Short Songs*, to sing and play to the lute, in 1600. An early copy in manuscript is in the Advocates' Library, Edinburgh. The accompaniment, arranged by the editor of this collection, is founded upon Morley's own bass part, written for the "Bass viole."

It will be observed how easily the song lends itself to duet singing, and one cannot but think that such was the original intention. The music is sung to the clown (Touchstone) and Audrey, whom he is about to marry, and is introduced into the play as follows:

Enter two Pages.

First Page. Well met, honest gentleman.

Touchstone. By my troth, well met. Come, sit, sit, and a song!

Second Page. We are for you: sit i' the middle.

First Page. Shall we clap into 't roundly, without hawking or spitting or saying we are hoarse, which are the only prologues to a bad voice?

Second Page. I' faith, i' faith; and both in a tune, like two gipsies on a horse.

Song follows.

Thomas Morley was born about 1557, and died 1604. In 1591 he was organist of St. Paul's Cathedral, and in 1592 Gentleman of the Chapel Royal. He studied under Byrd, and took his Mus. Bac. degree at Oxford in 1588. His compositions are of a melodious character, and many of his madrigals and "ballets" obtained great popularity. He wrote an admirable treatise entitled *A plaine and easie introduction to practicall musicke*, in form of a dialogue in three parts. This work was translated into German.

No. 11. *Where the bee sucks.*
From THE TEMPEST, *Act V, scene i.*
THIS song was composed by Robert Johnson, a composer and lutenist who flourished at the end of the sixteenth and beginning of the seventeenth centuries. He graduated at Oxford University as Mus. Bac. in 1597. In 1573–4 he was a retainer in the household of Sir Thomas Kytson, of Hengrave Hall, Suffolk. He subsequently came to London. Besides many books of "Ayres" for the "Lute and Bass Viole," and a

set of madrigals in three, four, five, six, seven, and eight parts, he composed music for the theatres, including a setting of the songs in *The Tempest* from which the editor has taken the two following numbers, viz. "Where the bee sucks" and "Full fathom five." At a later period Dr. John Wilson arranged these for three voices. Johnson also wrote music to the two dramas *The Witch* and *A Masque of the Gipsies*.

The editor feels convinced that Johnson wrote more music to Shakspere's words than is at present known, and thinks that careful search may result in discovering other interesting songs composed for other plays.

After being promised freedom Ariel sings "Where the bee sucks" while assisting Prospero to attire himself.

No. 12. *Full fathom five thy father lies.*
From THE TEMPEST, *Act I, scene ii.*
FOR a sketch of the composer see No. 11. Ariel sings this song to tell Prince Ferdinand that his father is drowned, though as a matter of fact he is alive and well.

No. 13. *Lawn as white as driven snow.*
From THE WINTER'S TALE, *Act IV, scene iv.*
THIS song is attributed to John Wilson, though some think it is by Robert Johnson. It is taken from Wilson's *Cheerful Ayres or Ballads, first composed for a single voice, and since set for three voices.* In this book of Wilson's are some songs by Johnson, "Full fathom five" being one of them; it is in fact printed under Johnson's name. The character of the music of "Lawn as white," and No. 14, "Take, O take," has a family likeness to Nos. 11 and 12. Special interest attaches to Dr. John Wilson, as it is generally supposed he was, as a boy, a singer at the theatre and was identical with the "Jackie Wilson" whose name appears in the Folio Edition of *Much Ado* instead of Balthaser, the character represented. If this conjecture be correct he would in all probability, as Ariel, sing Johnson's setting of "Where the bee sucks," which song Wilson afterwards included in this book of *Ayres*, printed in Oxford in

1659. Several of Shakspere's songs appear in his collections. Henry Lawes mentions him as a "great singer."

John Wilson was born in Kent in 1594, was made Mus. Doc. Oxon. in 1644, and was professor at that university 1656–62. In 1662 he was made a Gentleman of the Chapel Royal and Chamber Musician to Charles II. He composed many airs and ballads, besides church music and fantasias for viols. He died at Westminster in 1673.

The song "Lawn as white" is sung by Autolycus disguised as a pedlar.

No. 14. *Take, O take those lips away.*
From MEASURE FOR MEASURE, *Act IV, scene i.*
THIS song, though some attribute it to R. John-son, is considered to be by Dr. John Wilson, for particulars of whom see the details given in the previous notice.

If Dr. John Wilson was the "Jackie Wilson" mentioned in the Folio Edition previously alluded to, this song would in all probability be sung by him. Mariana in the play enters accompanied by a boy who sings "Take, O take those lips away." Mariana has been deserted by her false lover Angelo because her fortune was lost.

The song is truly a singer's song and is very beautiful, as in fact are all the examples given in this part; and they prove that the music performed in the plays during Shakspere's life was refined and artistic in character.

PART III. SETTINGS COMPOSED SINCE SHAKSPERE'S TIME TO THE MIDDLE OF THE NINETEENTH CENTURY

THIS part of the work consists of songs[1] composed after Shakspere's death, and extending to the middle of the nineteenth century, practically embracing a period of about two hundred years.

There would be no difficulty in collecting several hundred settings covered by the period. The editor, being limited, however, by space, has contented himself by including twenty-one only, selecting those he considered to be most characteristic and interesting.

No. 15. *Come unto these yellow sands.*
From THE TEMPEST, *Act I, scene ii. Composed by John Banister (1630–1679).*
JOHN BANISTER, a composer and violinist, was sent by Charles II to France to study; on his return he became leader of the king's band. He established a music school at Whitefriars, and gave concerts from 1672 to 1678. He composed music to Davenport's *Circe*, 1667. Later, together with P. Humfrey, he composed music to *The Tempest*, from which the song "Come unto these yellow sands" is taken. He also composed *Lessons for Viols*, songs, &c.

No. 16. *Where the bee sucks.*
From THE TEMPEST, *Act V, scene i. Composed by Pelham Humfrey (1647–1674).*
HUMFREY was one of the Children of the Chapel Royal, reëstablished after the Restoration. He showed much talent for composition at an early age, and in 1664 was sent by Charles II to study in Paris under Lulli. On his return he was appointed "Master of the Children" and Composer to His Majesty. He died at the early age of twenty-seven, and was buried in Westminster Abbey.

His works consist mostly of church music, odes and songs. He possessed ability of no ordinary type, and the advantages he received from his three years' study on the Continent are reflected in his own compositions and in the works of his pupil Henry Purcell.

An alteration in the text of the words of this song will be noticed.

No. 17. *The Willow Song.*
From OTHELLO, *Act IV, scene iii. Composed by Pelham Humfrey (1647–1674).*
SEE No. 16 for note about the composer. This

[1] *The songs in Parts III and IV are arranged chronologically by composer.*

very beautiful old song was written by Humfrey to the original words,—see note to No. 8,—but the editor found a version with the Shakspere text, the only variation being in the last two lines; he therefore feels no hesitation in including this song in the collection. It is found in Stafford Smith's *Musica Antiqua*.

No. 18. *Come unto these yellow sands.*
From THE TEMPEST, *Act I, scene ii. Composed by Henry Purcell* (1658–1695).
THE words of this song as set by Purcell are altered by Dryden.

This greatest and most original of English composers was (when about six years old) a chorister of the Chapel Royal, and is said to have written anthems while yet a chorister. In 1675, when but seventeen years old, he composed the opera of *Dido and Æneas*. In 1676 he wrote the music to Dryden's *Aurenge-Zebe*.

A copy of the music to *Macbeth*, usually credited to Mathew Lock, has been discovered in Purcell's handwriting; the manuscript is now in the possession of Dr. W. H. Cummings. Though Purcell would have been very young at the time, it appears more than probable that he was the composer of this music. The words not being by Shakspere, extracts from the work are not included in this collection.

In 1678 he wrote the overture and other music to Shadwell's alteration of Shakspere's *Timon of Athens*.

In 1680 he became organist of Westminster Abbey, and for six years gave up connection with theatres. In this interval it may be presumed that much of his church music was composed.

In 1682 he became organist of the Chapel Royal.

In 1690 Purcell composed new music for Shadwell's version of *The Tempest*. Two of the settings have retained uninterrupted possession of the stage from his time till this day, namely, those to "Full fathom five" and "Come unto these yellow sands."

In an opera composed during this year, *The Prophetess, or the history of Dioclesian*, Purcell made a great advance, calling into play larger orchestral resources than before. This opera was published in 1691, and in the dedication of it he says, "Musick and Poetry have ever been acknowledged sisters, and, walking hand in hand, support each other. As poetry is the harmony of words, so musick is that of notes; and as poetry is a rise above prose and oratory, so is musick the exaltation of poetry. Both may excel apart, but are most excellent when joined, for then they appear like wit and beauty in the same person. Poetry and painting have arrived to perfection in our own country; musick is still in its nonage, a forward child which gives hope of what it may be in England when the master of it shall find more encouragement. Being further from the sun, we are of later growth than our neighbour countries, and must be content to shake off our barbarity by degrees."

In 1691 Purcell wrote the music to *King Arthur* (amongst many others), and in 1692 to *The Fairy Queen* (an anonymous adaption of Shakspere's *Midsummer Night's Dream*) and Sir Charles Sedley's *Ode for the Queen's Birthday*; one of the airs in this last, viz. "May her blest example chase," has for its bass the air of the old song "Cold and Raw." The reason for this was, that Arabella Hunt and Gosling were once singing to Queen Mary, with Purcell as accompanist. After hearing several compositions by Purcell and others, the Queen asked Arabella Hunt to sing "Cold and Raw." Purcell, nettled at finding a common ballad preferred to his music, determined that the Queen should hear it again when she least expected it, and he adopted this ingenious method of effecting his object.

In addition to the settings Nos. 18 and 19 Purcell composed music to "Orpheus with his lute" and "Flout em," a catch for three voices.

A number of spurious songs introduced into the plays at this time are set by Purcell, among them being "Kind fortune smiles," "Dry those eyes," "Where does the black fiend," solo and chorus "In hell" and "Great Neptune."

Purcell died at his house in Dean's Yard, Westminster, on November 21, 1695.

No. 19. *Full fathom five thy father lies.*
From THE TEMPEST, *Act I, scene ii. Composed by Henry Purcell (1658–1695).*
[For comment see notes to No. 18.]

No. 20. *Who is Sylvia?*
From THE TWO GENTLEMEN OF VERONA, *Act IV, scene ii. Composed by Richard Leveridge (1670–1758).*
RICHARD LEVERIDGE, a bass vocalist and composer, sang in Drury Lane and Queen's theatres, 1705–12, and at Lincoln's Inn Fields and Covent Garden, 1713–30.

He composed music for the *Island Princess,* 1699, *Pyramus and Thisby,* 1716, and a collection of songs, two volumes, 1727. He is known as a song-writer, and by some is credited with the much discussed *Macbeth* music, on the authority of a notice in Rowe's edition of Shakspere. His best-known songs are "All in the downs" and "Roast beef of Old England." The example included in this collection well illustrates the style of his work. It has been wrongly attributed to Arne.

The song occurs in *The Two Gentlemen of Verona* under the following circumstance:

Julia, having reached the Emperor's city, in man's attire, is taken by her host to hear her faithless lover Protheus serenade Sylvia, the love of his friend Valentine, to whom he has turned traitor, in order that he may win Sylvia for himself.

No. 21. *Where the bee sucks.*
From THE TEMPEST, *Act V, scene i. Composed by Thomas Augustine Arne (1710–1778).*
THOMAS AUGUSTINE ARNE was the son of an upholsterer, and was born in King Street, Covent Garden. He was educated at Eton College, being intended for the legal profession, but his natural love for music led him to study privately. Several interesting stories are told of his many difficulties and ingenious devices to obtain lessons and opportunity for study.

He took lessons on the violin from Festing, and would occasionally borrow a livery in order to gain admission to the servants' gallery at the opera. He made such progress on the violin as to be able to lead a chamber band at the house of an amateur, who gave private concerts. There he was accidentally discovered by his father playing first violin. After fruitless efforts to induce his son to devote himself to the legal profession, the father gave up the attempt. Being free to practise openly, Arne soon, by his skill on the violin, charmed the whole family.

In 1738 he established his reputation as a lyric composer by the admirable manner in which he set Milton's *Comus.* In this he introduced a light, airy, original, and pleasing melody, wholly different from that of Purcell or Handel, whom all English composers had hitherto either pillaged or imitated. Indeed the melody of Arne at this time, and of his Vauxhall songs afterwards, forms an era in English music; it was so easy, natural, and agreeable to the whole kingdom that it had an effect upon the national taste; and till a more modern Italian style was introduced in the *pasticcio* English operas of Bickerstaff and Cumberland, Arne's was the standard of all perfection at our theatres and public gardens. (See Burney's *History,* vol. iv.)

On July 6, 1759, the University of Oxford created Arne Doctor of Music.

He composed a great number of admirable works chiefly for the theatre.

Dr. Arne was the first to introduce women's voices into oratorio choruses. This he did at Covent Garden Theatre, February 26, 1773, in a performance of his own, *Judith.*

The three songs introduced into this collection are good examples of his melodious and agreeable style.

No. 22. *When daisies pied and violets blue.*
From LOVE'S LABOR'S LOST, *Act V, scene ii. Composed by Thomas Augustine Arne (1710–1778).*
[For comment see note to No. 21.]

No. 23. *When icicles hang by the wall.*
From LOVE'S LABOR'S LOST, *Act V, scene ii. Composed by Thomas Augustine Arne (1710–1778).*
[For comment see note to No. 21.]

No. 24. *No more dams I'll make for fish.*
From THE TEMPEST, *Act II, scene ii. Composed by John Christopher Smith* (1712–1795).
APART from the character of the music of this song, some interest is attached to it as being composed by one who acted as Handel's amanuensis during the blindness of the great composer. His style, in most of his work, bears a great resemblance to that of his master. Smith's father, a German, acted as Handel's treasurer.

He composed two Shaksperian operas, *The Tempest* and *The Fairies,* an altered version of *A Midsummer Night's Dream.* Some editors have mistaken Smith's music for that of Purcell's,— Loder and Dr. Clarke, to wit.

No. 25. *She never told her love.*
From TWELFTH NIGHT, *Act II, scene iv. Composed by Franz Joseph Haydn* (1732–1809).
THE song is one of a set of six, dedicated to Lady Charlotte Bertie, and composed in 1795.

Franz Joseph Haydn, the father of the symphony and the quartet, was born at Rohrau, a small Austrian village. His parents both sang, and the child soon began to sing their simple songs.

On New Year's Day, 1791, Haydn came to London, where he was soon the object of every species of attention.

The culminating point of his reputation (not attained till he had reached old age) was the composition of the *Creation* and the *Seasons.* Of the *Creation* he says: "Never was I so pious. I knelt down every day, and prayed God to strengthen me in my work." This oratorio was first performed publicly in 1799, and produced an extraordinary impression. It was with reluctance that he composed music to the *Seasons,* for he knew his powers were failing, and the strain was too great. As he said afterwards, "The *Seasons* gave me the finishing stroke." He composed very little after this.

After a long seclusion, he appeared in public for the last time at a remarkable performance of the *Creation,* at the University of Vienna, on March 27, 1808. He was carried in his armchair to a place among the first ladies of the land. At the words, "And there was light," Haydn was quite overcome, and pointing upwards exclaimed, "It came from thence!" As the performance went on, his agitation became extreme, and it was thought better to take him home after the first part.

On May 26, 1809, he called his servants round him for the last time, and having been carried to the piano, solemnly played the *Emperor's Hymn* three times over. Five days afterwards he expired.

No. 26. *When that I was a little tiny boy.*
The Epilogue to TWELFTH NIGHT. *Composed by Joseph Vernon* (1738–1782).
THIS song is said to be by Joseph Vernon, who was a tenor vocalist born at Coventry. He studied under W. Savage, and appeared at Drury Lane Theatre in 1751.

He composed the music to *The Witches,* a pantomime, several songs and other vocal works. W. Linley has attributed this song to Fielding, but Dr. Rimbault proves that it was composed by Vernon, about 1760. Charles Knight says, "It is the most philosophical clown's song on record." Chappell thinks that the song is the original music. The character of the melody suggests that it might be.

No. 27. *Sigh no more, ladies.*
From MUCH ADO ABOUT NOTHING, *Act II, scene iii. Composed by R. J. S. Stevens* (1757–1837).
THE song is sung by Balthaser in the play, and in the *Shakspere Folio* instead of "enter Balthaser" appears "enter Jackie Wilson,"—a singer of the Burbage's Company, to which Shakspere belonged. Dr. Rimbault identifies the singer with Dr. John Wilson. (See previous notes on this subject.)

Richard John Samuel Stevens was born in London. He was trained as a chorister in St. Paul's Cathedral, under Savage, and became organist of the Temple Church in 1786, Charter House, 1796, Professor of Music, Gresham College, 1801. His death occurred in London.

His chief works were glees, of which he composed a great number. The song included in this book was originally composed as a glee, but it is so generally sung in the play arranged as a song that no collection of Shakspere's songs would be complete without its insertion.

No. 28. *Now the hungry lion roars.*
From A MIDSUMMER NIGHT'S DREAM, *Act V, scene i. Composed by William Linley (1767–1835).*
WILLIAM LINLEY, son of the composer Thomas Linley, was born at Bath, and educated at Harrow. He studied under Abel and his father. Later he was appointed to a post in the East India Company's service by Fox.

This notable amateur wrote *Shakspere's Dramatic Songs*, consisting of all the songs, duets and choruses in character, as introduced in his dramas. The song No. 28 is from that work. He composed two operas, glees, &c., and also wrote novels and other literary works.

No. 29. *If music be the food of love, play on.*
From TWELFTH NIGHT, *Act I, scene i. Composed by John Charles Clifton (1781–1841).*
THE editor has endeavored to include characteristic songs illustrating the period during which they were composed. This song, with its harp or piano accompaniment, is good of its kind, and shows a type of song much in vogue fifty or sixty years ago. Clifton was a pianist and composer of ability; he studied under R. Bellamy and Charles Wesley.

He wrote an opera called *Edwin*, many songs, glees, and a theory of harmony, besides other works.

No. 30. *Over hill, over dale.*
From A MIDSUMMER NIGHT'S DREAM, *Act II, scene i. Composed by Thomas Simpson Cook (1782–1848).*
THOMAS COOK, vocalist and composer, was born at Dublin. He studied under his father and Giordani. In 1803 he became conductor at a theatre in his native city and made his *début* as a vocalist in Storace's *Siege of Belgrade*. In 1813 he appeared in London and was appointed con-

ductor at Drury Lane Theatre. He wrote music to a number of plays, besides composing masses, glees, songs, solfeggi, &c. The words of "Over hill, over dale" were not written for music in the play, though they are good for the purpose. As an example of a florid soprano song it is excellent.

No. 31. *Bid me discourse.*
Sonnet from VENUS AND ADONIS, *Stanza xxiv. Composed by Sir Henry Rowley Bishop (1786–1855).*
SIR HENRY BISHOP was director of the music at Drury Lane Theatre in 1810, and became conductor in 1825; musical director in Vauxhall Gardens in 1830; Mus. Bac. Oxon. in 1839. He was knighted in 1842; Professor of Music at Oxford University, 1848; Mus. Doc. Oxon., 1853.

Bishop was a voluminous composer, and is now chiefly remembered by his songs and glees, and one opera, *Guy Mannering*. He composed music to a number of Shakspere's songs; perhaps he set more of them than any other composer. This, and the previous number, shows the influence of the florid Italian school, which was so popular at the time through the Italian operas. Though this song is not from the plays, it appears as a solo by Viola in Bishop's operatic version of *Twelfth Night*.

No. 32. *The Willow Song.*
From OTHELLO, *Act IV, scene iii. Composed by Gioachino Rossini (1792–1868).*
IT will be a matter of considerable interest to many to learn that Rossini composed a song to Shakspere's words, which can be rendered in English as effectively as in Italian. The song was composed for the opera *Otello*, in the year 1816, and is characteristic of the composer.

Rossini was the greatest, among the many great opera composers, of the first half of the nineteenth century.

No. 33. *Hark, hark! the lark.*
From CYMBELINE, *Act II, scene iii. Composed by Franz Schubert (1797–1828).*
SCHUBERT, born in Vienna, possessed wonderful

powers as a song-writer; in the opinion of many he ranks first in this branch of the musical art. He was the one great composer whose songs, regarded as a department of music, are absolutely his own,—full of dramatic fire, poetry, and pathos, with accompaniments of the utmost force, fitness, and variety.

Schubert lived in great poverty. " It is all but impossible to place one's self in the forlorn condition in which he must have resigned himself to his departure, and to realize the darkness of the valley of the shadow of death through which his simple, sincere, guileless soul passed to its last rest, and to the joyful resurrection and glorious renown which have since attended it." His works number one thousand, one hundred and thirty-one. He was by far the most prolific of composers. He wrote several operas, masses, symphonies, string quartets, and a multitude of pianoforte pieces and songs. Few, however, were published during his life, and these were miserably paid for. He sent three of his songs to Goethe in 1819, but the poet took no notice of the composer who was afterwards to give some of his songs a wider popularity than they could otherwise have enjoyed. Though Beethoven's stay in Vienna coincided for so many years with Schubert's lifetime, they only met twice. On the first occasion, Schubert's nervousness overcame him, and he rushed out of the room before he had written a word for the deaf Beethoven to read. On the second, Beethoven was hardly conscious, being then in his last illness. But some days before, he had become acquainted with a selection of Schubert's songs. These excited his admiration, and caused him to say, "Truly, Schubert has the divine fire."

Though Schubert's name was now becoming more widely known, he was still in poverty — sometimes on the brink of starvation. He died of typhus fever at the age of thirty-one. Of his many works only a small proportion was publicly performed during his life. Schumann was the first to force the world to listen to the treasures they had disregarded.

Schubert set only three of Shakspere's songs, "Come thou monarch of the vine," "Who is Sylvia?" and "Hark, hark! the lark." The last two are included in this collection.

No. 34. *Who is Sylvia?*
From THE TWO GENTLEMEN OF VERONA, *Act IV, scene ii. Composed by Franz Schubert* (1797–1828).
[See note to No. 33.]

No. 35. *Hark, hark! the lark.*
From CYMBELINE, *Act II, scene iii. Composed by Karl Friedrich Curschmann* (1805–1841).
CURSCHMANN'S fame rests on his powers as a song-writer; he is always melodious and natural, though never superficial or trivial.

As a child he showed great talent; he studied four years under Spohr and Hauptmann. His early death (thirty-six) cut short a career full of promise, for his future was bright in the extreme, and he doubtless bid fair to become one of the greatest of our song-writers.

This song is his only setting of Shakspere's words, and though interesting is not the best example of his gift which could be selected. He wrote the music to a German translation of Shakspere's words; a perverted translation then appeared in England under the title "Summer Morning." Mr. Greenhill restored Shakspere's words, which appear now for the first time in connection with this song.

Curschmann was a favorite song-composer before Schubert's songs were known. As a matter of chronology he comes after Schubert, but as a matter of style and development No. 35 should precede Nos. 33 and 34.

PART IV. RECENT SETTINGS

No. 36. *When that I was a little boy.*
The Epilogue to TWELFTH NIGHT. *Composed by Robert Schumann* (1810–1856).

SCHUMANN was one of the most original composers that ever lived; and even now his works are not generally understood and appreciated as they should be. He was born at Zwickau in Saxony; was educated at Leipzig for the law, but left the legal profession for music. His individuality of style, determined at the very outset, finds its most perfect expression in the smaller forms—piano-pieces and songs. In them he displays an artistic finish and a mastery of detail, which, united with poetic imagination and warmth of passion, are characteristic of his genius. He wrote a great number of songs, the best of which are unsurpassed for depth of emotional expression and delicate fancy. It is interesting to find that in 1851 Schumann composed music to verses by Shakspere. He used, however, a German translation, which made it necessary to change slightly the original English words in fitting them to his music.

No. 37. *Autolycus' Song.*
From A WINTER'S TALE, *Act IV, scene iv. Composed by James Greenhill* (1840–   ).

THE song in this collection is a fine example of the composer's work, and critics have pronounced it one of the best settings of these words. Mr. Greenhill, who was born in London, is a well-known vocalist, composer and teacher. For about twenty years he was choirmaster for the late Rev. H. R. Haweis, and he was also director of music for the New Shakspere Society during the five years of its existence.

No. 38. *Sigh no more, ladies.*
From MUCH ADO ABOUT NOTHING, *Act II, scene iii. Composed by Sir Arthur Seymour Sullivan* (1842–1900).

BORN in London, Sullivan was till 1857 a chorister in the Chapel Royal. He was elected Mendelssohn Scholar at the Royal Academy of Music in 1856, and in 1858 went to Leipzig to study, returning in 1861. While there he composed his music to *The Tempest.*

Sullivan composed many serious and elevated works, such as *Ivanhoe, The Golden Legend, The Light of the World, The Prodigal Son,* a *Symphony in E,* &c. In later years his series of light operas, beginning with *Pinafore,* established a reputation which will perhaps outlive that made by his serious works.

Sullivan composed a great number of successful songs and church music. The song "Sigh no more, ladies," included in this collection, was written for Sims Reeves, and has a certain interest connected with it, inasmuch as it is engraved from a copy altered and improved by Sir Arthur, and is therefore probably the only edition published exactly as he wished it sung, after the experience of hearing it performed by Mr. Sims Reeves.

No. 39. *Fear no more the heat o' the sun.*
From CYMBELINE, *Act IV, scene ii. Composed by Sir C. Hubert H. Parry* (1848–   ).

A GIFTED and voluminous composer, Parry's works are distinguished by their directness and verve. His style is broadly melodious, and yet abounds in evidences of clever contrapuntal skill. The choral ode "Blest Pair of Syrens" is perhaps his most popular work.

Sir Hubert Parry was born at Bournemouth. He is Professor of Music at Oxford University, and Principal of the Royal College of Music, London. Song No. 39 was specially composed for this volume.

No. 40. *Who is Sylvia?*
From THE TWO GENTLEMEN OF VERONA, *Act IV, scene ii. Composed by Monk Gould* (1858–   ).

MR. GOULD is the composer of a large number of songs, some of which have become very popular, notably "The Curfew," "Daybreak," "The Banshee," "Jacobite Ballads," "Cavalier Ballads," &c. He has also composed much church music, and was till lately the organist and choir-master of St. Michael's Church, Portsmouth, and conductor of the Philharmonic Society, Portsmouth. He was born at Tavistock, Devon.

No. 41. *Blow, blow, thou winter wind.*
From AS YOU LIKE IT, *Act II, scene vii. Composed by William Arms Fisher* (1861–).
MR. FISHER was born in San Francisco, California, where he studied harmony, organ and piano with John P. Morgan. He later studied singing with William Shakespeare in London; and on his return to New York he became a pupil of Parker in counterpoint and fugue, and of Dvořák in composition and instrumentation. He was instructor in harmony for several years at the National Conservatory, until, in 1895, he went to Boston, where he now lives.

Mr. Fisher's creative activity has been chiefly in the field of lyric composition, and many of his songs have become very successful. They are varied in mood, but uniformly well thought from the singer's standpoint, and he secures his effects without violating the canons of good vocal art.

No. 42. *Sigh no more, ladies.*
From MUCH ADO ABOUT NOTHING, *Act II, scene iii. Composed by William Arms Fisher* (1861–).
[See note to No. 41.]

No. 43. *It was a lover and his lass.*
From AS YOU LIKE IT, *Act V, scene iii. Composed by Gerard Barton* (1861–).
BORN at Fundenhall, Norfolk, England, Mr. Barton studied the organ under Dr. Edward Bunnett and Sir Walter Parratt, and composition with Dr. J. Varley Roberts. In 1884 he went to America, where he finally settled on the Pacific coast as a professional musician. He has held the position of organist in churches at Los Angeles, Santa Barbara and San Francisco; and is at present (1905) at the head of the musical department of Oahu College, and organist of St. Andrew's Cathedral, Honolulu. The list of Mr. Barton's compositions includes many songs, both

sacred and secular, a setting of the mass, part-songs, etc.

No. 44. *Orpheus with his lute.*
From HENRY THE EIGHTH, *Act III, scene i. Composed by Carl Busch* (1862–).
MR. BUSCH was born at Bjerre, Jutland, Denmark. He studied music in the Conservatorium of Copenhagen, and later at the Conservatorium of Brussels, and under Godard in Paris. He lives at present in Kansas City, where he is conductor of the Philharmonic Society and the Oratorio Society.

Mr. Busch has written a number of large works for orchestra, and for chorus with orchestra,—notably the cantatas *The League of the Alps* and *King Olaf*. Besides these he is the composer of many songs, anthems and part-songs.

No. 45. *Under the greenwood tree.*
From AS YOU LIKE IT, *Act II, scene v. Composed by Carl Busch* (1862–).
[See note to No. 44.]

No. 46. *And let me the canakin clink.*
From OTHELLO, *Act II, scene iii. Composed by Harvey Worthington Loomis* (1865–).
MR. LOOMIS was born in Brooklyn, New York, and has received his entire musical training in New York City, where he now lives. He studied composition under Dvořák, the piano with Mme. Madeline Schiller. Fluent melody and a rich and daring harmonic sense are evident in his compositions. Besides a host of songs and piano pieces, he has won distinction in the unusual field of pantomimic music, in the higher sense of the word. On somewhat similar lines are the "musical backgrounds" intended to illuminate the recitation of some poem.

Mr. Loomis has set to music a large number of Shakspere's songs, of which Nos. 46 and 47 are noteworthy examples.

No. 47. *Crabbed age and youth.*
From THE PASSIONATE PILGRIM, *xii. Composed by Harvey Worthington Loomis* (1865–).
[See note to No. 46.]

No. 48. *Orpheus with his lute.*
From HENRY THE EIGHTH, *Act III, scene i. Composed by Charles Fonteyn Manney (1872–   ).*
MR. MANNEY was born in Brooklyn, New York, where he was for several years a boy-chorister. He began the study of music with William Arms Fisher, and later, on his removal to Boston, where he now lives, he became a pupil of Wallace Goodrich and Dr. Percy Goetschius. He is the composer of various anthems, part-songs, and piano pieces; a comic opera and two sacred cantatas; besides many songs, which show marked lyric feeling, and a graceful and rich melodic vein.

No. 49. *It was a lover and his lass.*
From AS YOU LIKE IT, *Act V, scene iii. Composed by H. Clough-Leighter (1874–   ).*
FROM an early age a pupil of his mother, and later of Dr. J. Humfrey Anger in Toronto, Mr. Clough-Leighter, who was born in Washington, D. C., has received his entire musical training in America. As a boy he sang in a vested choir, and at fifteen he was a professional organist. He has since held several posts as organist and choral director. He has written various church services, anthems and choral works; besides many songs, which evince rich and free harmonic thought, and a real lyricism. Mr. Clough-Leighter at present lives in Boston.

No. 50. *O mistress mine.*
From TWELFTH NIGHT, *Act II, scene iii. Composed by Samuel Coleridge-Taylor (1875–   ).*
THIS gifted, all-round musician and composer was born in London, where he was one of the singing-boys in St. George's Church, Croydon. He later became a student at the Royal College of Music, and afterwards was a pupil of Sir Charles Villiers Stanford. He is now actively engaged as a teacher in Trinity College, London, and as conductor of the Handel Society, London, and the Rochester Choral Society. His most important works are a *Symphony in A minor;* a setting of portions of Longfellow's *Hiawatha* for solos, chorus and orchestra; an oratorio, *The Atonement,* &c. Mr. Coleridge-Taylor is also the composer of several songs, and some interesting piano pieces based upon negro melodies.

APPENDIX

HEREWITH are given the original versions of several songs included in this volume, which may be of interest for purposes of comparison; likewise some additional old melodies referred to by Shakspere. Our modern scale, so utterly different to the modes in vogue at that early period, and the instrument which plays the accompaniment at the present time being also entirely unlike any with which the old composers were familiar, are sufficient reasons of justification for such harmonic and other changes as the editor deemed advisable.

HEART'S EASE

From Playford's English Dancing Master, page 54 (1650)

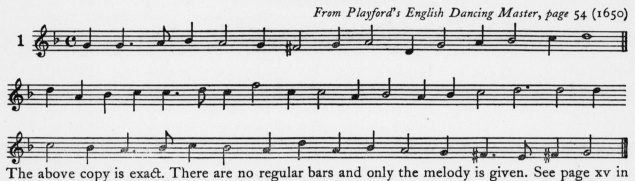

The above copy is exact. There are no regular bars and only the melody is given. See page xv in Notes on the Songs and page 9 of the music.

The following is the melody of "Hartes ease" from an MS. Lute Book (page 84) in the Cambridge University Library, Dd. 2. 11.

O MISTRIS MYNE

From Fitzwilliam Virginal Book, No. 66   *As arranged by William Byrd*

Song from *Twelfth Night*; see page xvi in Notes on the Songs and page 22 of the music. The strokes through the note-stems indicate a tremblant 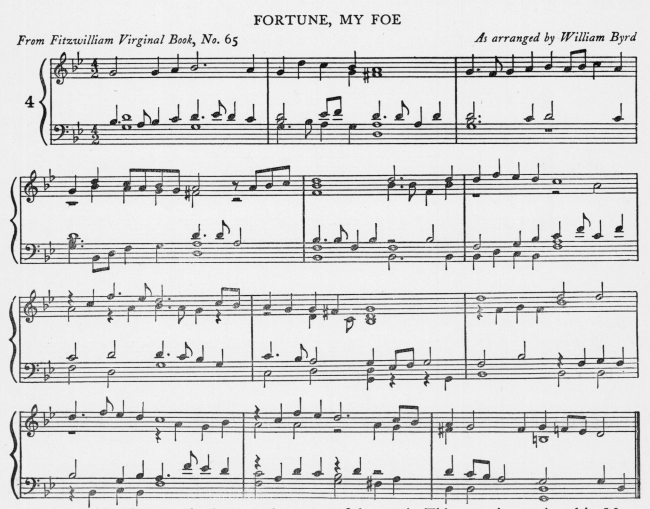.

FORTUNE, MY FOE

From Fitzwilliam Virginal Book, No. 65   *As arranged by William Byrd*

See page xvi in Notes to the Songs and page 13 of the music. This song is mentioned in *Merry Wives of Windsor*, Act III. Scene 3. To this air was sung also the old ballad of *Titus Andronicus* upon which Shakspere founded his play of the same name.

WATKINS ALE

From Fitzwilliam Virginal Book, No. 180

Anonymous

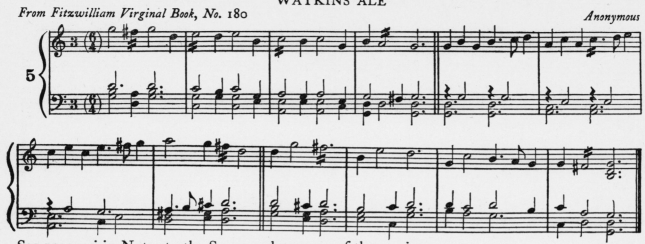

See page xvi in Notes to the Songs and page 17 of the music.

ADDITIONAL OLD MELODIES REFERRED TO BY SHAKSPERE

A ROUND

Quoted from Hawkins

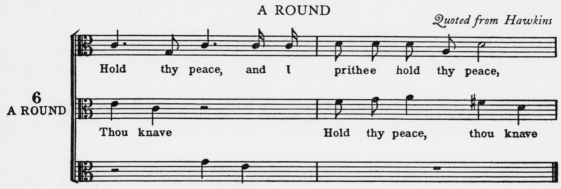

Hold thy peace, and I prithee hold thy peace,

Thou knave   Hold thy peace, thou knave

Thou knave

See *Twelfth Night*, Act ii. Scene 3.

JOG ON, JOG ON THE FOOTPATH WAY

Hawkins. From Fitzwilliam Virginal Book

Richard Farnaby

Repeat
with
Ornaments

See *Winter's Tale*.

FAREWELL, DEAR LOVE

(Published in 1601)

From "Songs and Ayres set out for the Lute," Book I

ROBERT JONES
Edited and arranged by Dr. Charles Vincent

*) The poem has three more verses.

ML-1206-2

PEG O' RAMSAY

Verses from
"Wit and Mirth" (1719)

Ancient Melody from
Dr. Bull MSS
Edited and arranged by Dr. Charles Vincent

*There are two more verses.

ML-1207-2

*) The final chord in parentheses might be omitted at the end of the song, the voice part ending on **A.**

GREEN-SLEEVES

(Composed during the reign of Henry VIII)

Ancient Melody
from W. Ballet's "Lute Book"
Edited and arranged by Dr. Charles Vincent

1. A - las, my love,— ye do me wrong, To
2. I have been read - y at your hand, To

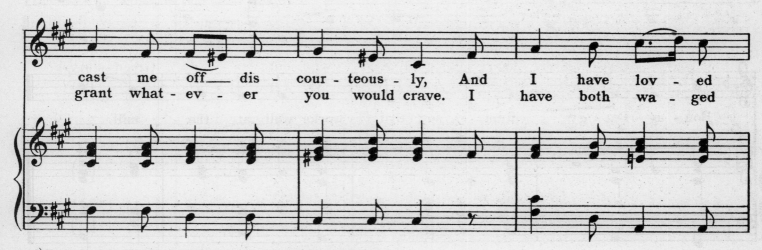

cast me off— dis - cour - teous - ly, And I have lov - ed
grant what - ev - er you would crave. I have both wa - ged

*) For remaining stanzas of the poem see the Notes to Part I.

ML-1208-2

you so long,— De - light - ing in — your com - pa - ny.
life and land,— Your love— and good - will for to have.

With good accent

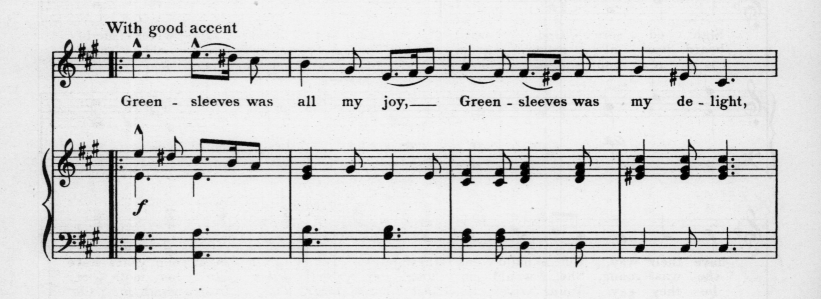

Green - sleeves was all my joy,—— Green - sleeves was my de - light,

Repeat last eight measures as a Chorus

Green - sleeves was my heart of gold, And who but la - dy Green - sleeves?

HEIGH-HO! FOR A HUSBAND

Verses slightly altered from
"Wit and Mirth"(1719)

Ancient melody from
John Gamble's MS "Common-place Book"
Edited and arranged by Dr. Charles Vincent

ML-1209-2

die a maid, A - pol - lo is for - sworn. Heigh - ho!
needs must have And this was still her cry: "Heigh - ho!
have their will, 'Tis best to die a maid. Heigh - ho!

for a hus - band, Heigh - ho! for a hus - band," Still this was her
for a hus - band, Heigh - ho! for a hus - band," Still this was her
with a hus - band, Heigh - ho! with a hus - band, What a life lead

song, "I will have a hus - band, have a hus - band, Be
song, "I will have a hus - band, have a hus - band, Be
I! Out up - on a hus - band, such a hus - band, fie,

he old or young."
he old or young."
fie, fie, Oh! fie."

1.&2. D.S. 3.

D.S.

HEART'S EASE

Ancient Melody
16th Century or earlier
Edited and arranged by Dr. Charles Vincent

ML.-4210-2

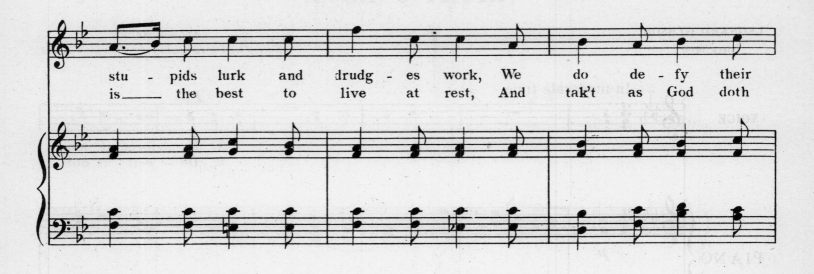

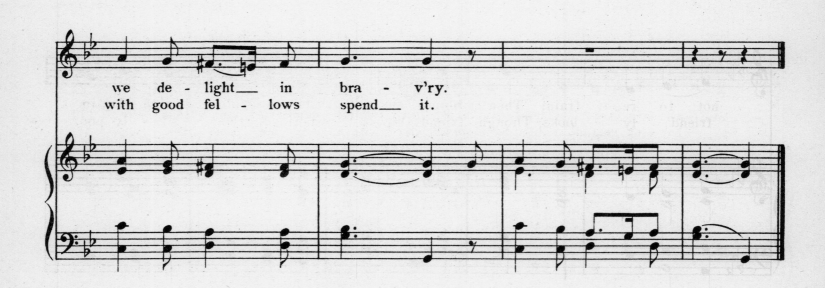

LIGHT O' LOVE

LEONARD GYBSON
(circa 1570)

Ancient Melody
Edited and arranged by Dr. Charles Vincent

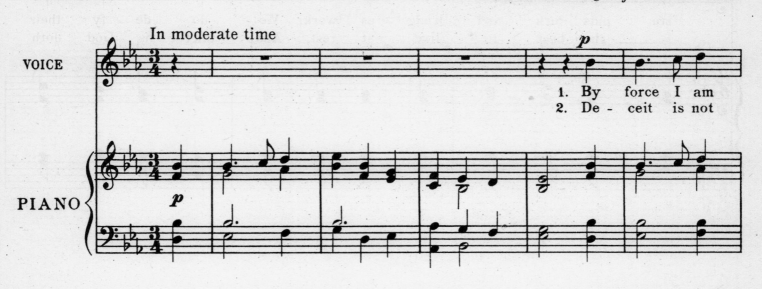

1. By force I am
2. De - ceit is not

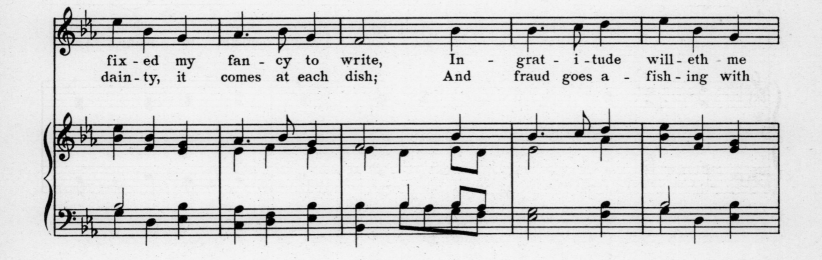

fix - ed my fan - cy to write, In - grat - i -tude will - eth me
dain - ty, it comes at each dish; And fraud goes a - fish - ing with

not to re - frain; Then blame me not, la - dies, al - though I in -
friend - ly looks; Though friend - ship is spoil - ed, the sil - ly poor

ML - 1211 - 2

dite   What light - ly love   now___ a - mongst you doth   reign. Your
fish   That   hov - er and   shiv - er up - on   your false   hooks; With

tra - ces in   pla - ces, with   out - ward al   - lure - ments, Doth   move___ my en -
bait you lay   wait___ to   catch here and   there___ Which   caus - es poor

deavour to   be the more plain; Your ni - cings and   ti - cings, with   sun - dry pro -
fish - es their free - dom to   lose. Then lout ye and flout ye, where - by doth ap -

cure - ments, To   pub - lish yon   light - ie love   doth me con - strain.
pear___ Your   light - y love   la - dies, still   cloak - ed with   gloss.

THREE MERRY MEN BE WE

Trio for Two Tenors and a Bass

Several old tunes
Edited and arranged by Dr. Charles Vincent

ML-1212-6

this she does When she pleas-es to pal-ter, In-

stead of his wa-ges She gives him a hal-ter.

Refrain
Lively

Three mer-ry men, And three mer-ry men, And three mer-ry men are we, As

Repeat refrain **pp**

e'er did sing Three parts in a string, All un-der the tri-ple tree.

15

ML-1212-6

in I have my wish - es, That I, who at so man - y a feast Have pleas'd so man - y

tast-ers, Should come my-self for to be dress'd A dish for you, my mas-ters.

Refrain
Lively

Three mer- ry men, And three mer-ry men, Oh, three mer-ry men are we, As

e'er did sing Three parts in a string, All un - der the green-wood tree.

The Pantler (*1st Tenor*)

Moderato

O man or beast, or you at least, That

(*"Watkins' Ale"*)

wears or brow or ant-ler, Prick up your ears un-to the tears Of me poor Paul the

pant-ler. That am thus chipt be-cause I clipt The curs-ed crust of trea-son

With loy-al knife, O dole-ful strife, To hang me thus with-out rea-son.

Three mer-ry men, And three mer-ry men, Oh, three mer-ry men are
we, That e'er did sing Three parts in a string, All
un-der the tri-ple tree, All un-der the tri-ple tree.

THE WILLOW SONG

WILLIAM SHAKSPERE
From "Othello," Act IV, Scene 3

Melody from
Thomas Dallis's "Lute-Book" (1583)
Edited and arranged by Dr. Charles Vincent

ML-1213-3

wil-low, wil-low, wil-low, wil-low! My gar-land shall be; Sing all a green

wil-low, wil-low, wil-low, wil-low, Sing all a green

wil-low, My gar-land shall be. The

fresh streams ran by her, and mur-mur'd her moans; Sing wil-low, willow,

O MISTRESS MINE

WILLIAM SHAKSPERE
From "Twelfth Night," Act II, Scene 3

Melody from
Queen Elizabeth's Virginal Book (1611)
Edited and arranged by Dr. Charles Vincent

ML.-1214-2

IT WAS A LOVER AND HIS LASS

WILLIAM SHAKSPERE
From "As You Like It," Act V, Scene 3

THOMAS MORLEY (circa 1557-1604)
Edited and arranged by Dr. Charles Vincent

ML-1215-2

spring-time, the on-ly pret-ty ring-time, When birds do sing,hey ding-a-ding a-ding, hey

ding-a-ding-a-ding, hey ding-a-ding-a-ding,Sweet lov-ers love the spring,In spring-time,

In spring-time, the on-ly pret-ty ring-time, When birds do sing, hey

ding-a-ding-a-ding,hey ding-a-ding-a-ding, hey ding-a-ding-a-ding,Sweet lov-ers love the spring.

WHERE THE BEE SUCKS

WILLIAM SHAKSPERE
From "The Tempest," Act V, Scene I

ROBERT JOHNSON (circa 1590)
Edited and arranged by Dr. Charles Vincent

ML-1216-2

FULL FATHOM FIVE THY FATHER LIES

WILLIAM SHAKSPERE
From "The Tempest," Act I, Scene 2

ROBERT JOHNSON (circa 1590)
Edited and arranged by Dr. Charles Vincent

ML.-1217-2

rich and strange. Sea-nymphs hour-ly ring his knell: Hark! now I hear them, Hark!

now I hear them, ding - dong, bell. Ding-dong, ding-dong, bell,

Ding-dong, ding-dong, bell, Ding-dong, ding-dong, bell, Ding-dong, ding-dong,

bell, Ding-dong, ding-dong, bell, Ding-dong, ding-dong, bell.

LAWN AS WHITE AS DRIVEN SNOW

WILLIAM SHAKSPERE
From "A Winter's Tale," Act IV, Scene 4

JOHN WILSON (1594-1673)
or ROBERT JOHNSON (circa 1590)
Edited and arranged by Dr. Charles Vincent

ML-1218-2

Pins and pok-ing sticks, pins and pok-ing sticks, and pok-ing sticks of steel;

What maids lack, what maids lack, what maids lack from head to heel,

What maids lack from head to heel. Come buy of me, come,

come buy, come buy. Buy, lads! or else your lasses cry; Come buy!

TAKE, O TAKE THOSE LIPS AWAY

WILLIAM SHAKSPERE
From "Measure for Measure," Act IV, Scene I.

JOHN WILSON (1594-1673)
Edited and arranged by Dr. Charles Vincent

Take,___ O take those lips___ a - way, That so

sweet - ly were for - sworn; And those eyes, the___ break of day,

Lights that do mis - lead the morn: But my kiss - es bring a - gain;

Seals of___ love, but seal'd in vain.

MI.-1219-1

COME UNTO THESE YELLOW SANDS

(Published in 1670)

WILLIAM SHAKSPERE
From "The Tempest," Act I, Scene 2

JOHN BANISTER (1630-1679)
Edited and arranged by Dr. Charles Vincent

M L-1220-2

A little quicker.

Foot it feat - ly here and there; And, sweet sprites, the

burth - en bear: Hark! hark! Bow wow, The watch - dogs bark, Bow-wow,

Hark! hark! I hear The strain of strut - ting chan - ti -

cleer Cry, Cock - a - doo - dle - doo.

WHERE THE BEE SUCKS

WILLIAM SHAKSPERE
From "The Tempest," Act V, Scene I

PELHAM HUMFREY (1647-1674)
Edited and arranged by Dr. Charles Vincent

Where the bee sucks, there lurk I; In a cow-slip's bell I lie; There I ___ couch when owls ___ do ___ cry, On the swal-low's wings I fly, Af - ter sun - set mer - ri - ly. mer - ri - ly.

ML-1221-2

THE WILLOW SONG

(Composed in 1678)

WILLIAM SHAKSPERE
From "Othello," Act IV, Scene 3

PELHAM HUMFREY (1647-1674)
Edited and arranged by Dr. Charles Vincent

The poor soul sat sigh-ing by a sy-ca-more tree, Sing all a green wil-low; Her hand on her bo-som, her head on her knee, Sing wil-low, wil-low, sing wil-low, wil-low.

ML-1222-3

The fresh streams ran by her, And mur - mur'd her moans; Her salt tears fell from her, and soft - en'd the stones; Sing wil - low, wil - low, sing wil - low, wil - low.

Come, all ye for - sak - en, and _____ mourn now with me; Who speaks of a false love, Mine's fals - er than he. Sing wil - low, wil - low, sing wil - low, wil - low.

COME UNTO THESE YELLOW SANDS

WILLIAM SHAKSPERE
From "The Tempest" Act I, Scene 2

HENRY PURCELL
(1658-1695)

Come un - to these yel - - - low sands, And then take hands,

Come un - to_ these yel - - - low sands, And then take hands;

Foot it feat - ly here and there, And let the rest the bur - then bear.

ML-1223-2

Foot it feat - ly here and there, And let the rest the __ bur - then bear.

Hark! hark! The watch - dogs bark; Hark! hark! I hear __ The strain of chan - ti - cleer,

Hark! hark! I hear __ The strain of chan - ti - cleer. Hark! hark! The watch - dogs bark;

Hark! hark! I hear The strain of chan - ti - cleer, Hark! hark! I hear __ The strain of chan - ti - cleer.

FULL FATHOM FIVE THY FATHER LIES

WILLIAM SHAKSPERE
From "The Tempest," Act I, Scene 2

HENRY PURCELL
(1658-1695)

Oliver Ditson Company

ML-1224-3

44

suf-fer, doth suf-fer a sea - - change In-to some - thing rich__ and strange.

Sea - nymphs hour - ly ring his knell; Hark! now I hear them, ding-dong, ding-dong, bell.__

8ves sempre

Hark! now I hear them, ding-dong, ding-dong, bell.__ Hark! now I hear__them, hark! now I hear them,

8ves sempre

hark! now I hear__them, ding - dong, bell, ding, ding-dong, bell, ding - dong, bell.

WHO IS SYLVIA?

WILLIAM SHAKSPERE
From "The Two Gentlemen of Verona," Act IV, Scene 2

RICHARD LEVERIDGE (1670-1758)
Edited and arranged by Dr. Charles Vincent

ML-1225-4

mi - - red be. be. Is she

kind as she ____ is fair? For beau-ty lives ____ with kind-ness.

Love doth to __ her __ eyes __ re-pair, To help __ him __ of __ his __

blind-ness; and be- ing help'd, in-ha- bits there.

48

her let us gar - lands bring, To her let us gar - lands

bring. She ex - cels each mor - tal thing, Up -

on the dull earth dwell - ing: To her let us gar - lands

bring, To her let us gar - lands bring.

ML-1225-4

WHERE THE BEE SUCKS

WILLIAM SHAKSPERE
From "The Tempest," Act V, Scene I

THOMAS AUGUSTINE ARNE (1710-1778)
Edited and arranged by Dr. Charles Vincent

ML-1226-3

cry. On a bat's back do I fly

Af - ter sun - set mer - ri - ly,

rall.

mer - ri - ly, Af - ter sun - set mer - ri - ly.

ly.

rall.

a tempo

Mer - ri - ly, mer-ri-ly shall I live now Un - der the blos-som that hangs on the

bough. Mer-ri-ly, mer-ri-ly shall I live now Un-der the blos-som that hangs on the

bough, Un - der the blos - som that hangs on the bough.

WHEN DAISIES PIED AND VIOLETS BLUE
(THE CUCKOO SONG)

WILLIAM SHAKSPERE
From "Love's Labor's Lost," Act V, Scene 2

THOMAS AUGUSTINE ARNE (1710-1778)
Edited by Dr. Charles Vincent

ML-1227-4

cuc-koo then, on ev-'ry tree, Hails the sweet spring, hails the sweet spring,

rit. *p* *cresc.*

hails the sweet spring, and thus sings he, Cuc-koo, cuc-koo, cuc-koo,

colla voce *p* *cresc.*

f.

cuc-koo, cuc-koo; Oh, pleas-ing sound, oh, pleas-ing sound, While

f

rit. *tr* *tr*

ech-o an-swers far a-round, While ech-o an-swers far a-

round.

When shep-herds pipe on oat-en straws, And mer-ry larks are

plough-men's clocks, When tur-tles pair, and rooks, and daws, And fields are scat-ter'd

o'er with flocks. The cuc-koo then, on ev-'ry tree, Hails the sweet spring,

hails the sweet spring, hails the sweet spring, and thus sings he, Cuc-koo, cuc-koo, cuc-koo,

cuc-koo, cuc-koo, Oh, pleas - ing sound, oh, pleas - ing sound, While

ech - o an-swers far a-round, While ech-o an-swers far a-round.

WHEN ICICLES HANG BY THE WALL
(THE OWL)

WILLIAM SHAKSPERE
From "Love's Labor's Lost," Act V, Scene 2

THOMAS AUGUSTINE ARNE
(1710-1778)

Tom bears logs in - to ___ the hall, And milk comes fro - zen
home in pail;
When blood is nipp'd and
ways ___ be foul, Then night - ly sings the star - ing owl,
Then night - ly sings the star - ing owl, To -

whit, tu - whoo, _____ tu - whoo, _____ A

mer - ry, mer - ry note, A mer - ry, mer - ry

note, While greas - y Joan, greas - y Joan, While

greas - y Joan _ doth keel the pot.

When loud_ the wind_doth blow, And cough - ing drowns the par - son's saw, And birds sit brood-ing in_ the snow, And Ma-rian's nose_ looks red_ and raw; When roast-ed crabs hiss in_ the bowl, Then night-ly sings the star-ing owl,

Then night - ly sings the star - ing owl, Tu-whit, tu - whoo _____

tu - whoo, _____ A mer-ry, mer-ry note, A

mer-ry, mer-ry note, While greas - y Joan, greas - y Joan, While

greas - y Joan _ doth keel the pot.

NO MORE DAMS I'LL MAKE FOR FISH

(CALIBAN'S SONG)

WILLIAM SHAKSPERE
From "The Tempest," Act II, Scene 2

JOHN CHRISTOPHER SMITH
(1712-1795)

Oliver Ditson Company

M L-1229-3

man!

No more dams_ I'll make_ for fish, No more dams_ I'll make_ for

fish, Nor_ fetch fir - ing, At _ re - quir - ing, Nor scrape trench-er, Nor_ wash

colla voce

dish, No more dams I'll make for fish, Nor fetch fir - ing, At _ re-

SHE NEVER TOLD HER LOVE

WILLIAM SHAKSPERE
From "Twelfth Night" Act II, Scene 4

FRANZ JOSEPH HAYDN
(1732-1809)

Largo assai e con espressione

PIANO

She nev - er told her love, she nev - er told her___

Oliver Ditson Company

ML-1230-3

love   But let con-ceal-ment,   like a   worm   in   the

bud,   Feed   on   her   dam   ask

cheek.

She

WHEN THAT I WAS A LITTLE TINY BOY

WILLIAM SHAKSPERE
The Epilogue to "Twelfth Night"

JOSEPH VERNON (1738-1782)
Edited and arranged by Dr. Charles Vincent

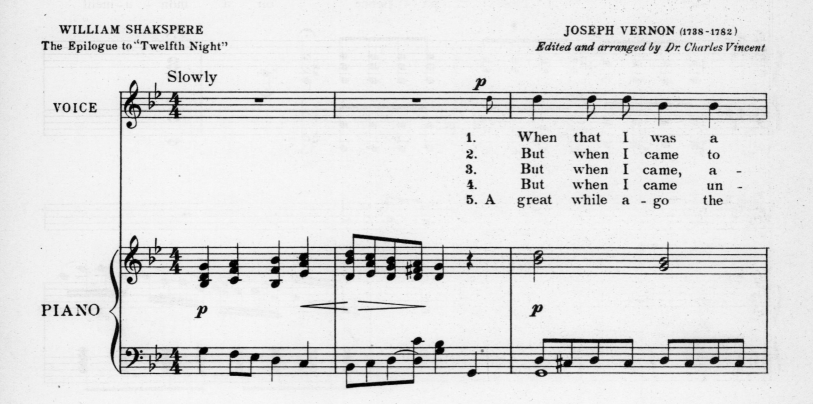

1. When that I was a
2. But when I came to
3. But when I came, a-
4. But when I came un-
5. A great while ago the

lit-tle ti-ny boy,
man's es-tate,
las! to wive,
to my bed,
world be-gun,

With a hey, ho! the wind and the rain,

A
'Gainst
By
With
But

68

ML-1231-2

SIGH NO MORE, LADIES

WILLIAM SHAKSPERE
From "Much Ado About Nothing," Act II, Scene 3

R. J. S. STEVENS (1757-1837)
Edited and arranged by Dr. Charles Vincent

M I.-1232 - 4

70

Then sigh not so, but let them go, And be you blithe and bon - ny, And be you_ blithe_ and_ bon - ny, Con - vert - ing_ all your_ sounds of_ woe, Con - vert - ing_ all your_ sounds of_ woe To Hey non - ny, non - ny, Hey non - ny, non - ny, Hey non - ny, non - ny, Hey non - ny, non - ny.

colla voce

Sing no more dit - ties, la - dies, sing no more__ Of dumps so__ dull and heav - y, Of dumps so__ dull and heav - y; The fraud of men was ev - er so,__ Since sum-mer first was leav-y, Since summer__first was leav - y. Then sigh not so, but let them

go, And be you blithe and bon-ny, And be you blithe and

bon-ny; Con - vert - ing all your sounds of woe, Con - vert - ing all your

sounds of woe, To Hey non-ny, non-ny, Hey non-ny, non-ny, Hey non-ny,

non-ny, Hey non-ny, non-ny.

NOW THE HUNGRY LION ROARS

WILLIAM SHAKSPERE
From "A Midsummer Night's Dream"
Act V, Scene I

WILLIAM LINLEY (1767-1835)
Edited by Dr. Charles Vincent

Now the hun-gry li - on — roars, And the wolf be - howls the moon; — Whilst the heav - y plough - man snores, All with wear-y task for - done, — All with wear - y — task for - done. Now the

ML.-1233-4

wast-ed brands do glow, Whilst the screech - owl, screech-ing loud,_ Puts the

wretch, that lies in woe,_ In re - mem-brance of_ a_ shroud. Now it

is the time of night, That the graves, all gap-ing wide, Ev - 'ry

one lets forth its sprite, In_ the_ church-way paths to glide.

Now the king of ter - ror_ reigns O - ver ci - ty, o - ver fold;_ Fright - ing hum - ble rus - tic swains, And the lord of wealth un - told,_ And the lord of_ wealth un - told. Now the mi - ser, full_ of _ care, Bars and

dou - ble - locks his   door, __ That   no strang - er may have   share __ In his

rich but use - less   store. Vain, for soon al - migh - ty Death   Casts his

rich - es. to the wind,   Wrecks his pal - ace with   a   breath,   Hides at

once his name and   kind.

IF MUSIC BE THE FOOD OF LOVE, PLAY ON

WILLIAM SHAKSPERE
From "Twelfth Night," Act I, Scene I

JOHN CHARLES CLIFTON
(1781-1841)

ML-1234-5

sound   that   breathes   up-on a bank of   vi - o-lets,

steal - - - ing,   steal - - - ing,

and_____ giv - - ing   o - - dour

like   the sweet   sound   up - -

on__ a bank of vi - o-lets, like the sweet

sound, the sweet__ sound, that

breathes up-on a bank of vi - - - o-lets,

ad lib. *cresc.* *dim.* *dim.* *colla voce* *lentando*

Andante

steal - - -ing, steal - - -ing,

sempre legato

and___ giv - ing o - dour steal - - ing,

steal - - ing, and___ giv-ing o - dour.

E - nough; no_ more.

OVER HILL, OVER DALE

WILLIAM SHAKSPERE
From "A Midsummer Night's Dream"
Act II, Scene I

THOMAS SIMPSON COOK
(1782-1848)

Allegro vivace e spiritoso

PIANO

O - ver hill,   o - ver dale,   Tho-rough bush,   Tho-rough briar, O - ver

park,   o - ver pale,   Tho-rough flood,   Tho-rough fire, O - ver hill,   o - ver dale,   Tho-rough

ML - 1235 - 8

bush, Tho-rough briar, O-ver park, o-ver pale, Tho-rough flood, Tho-rough fire, I do

wan - - - - - - - - - der ev - - 'ry

cresc. *poco a poco* *f* *ff*

where, Swift-er than the moon's sphere,

p

Swift - er than the moon's sphere; And I serve, I serve the

fair - y queen, To dew her orbs up - on the green.

Swift - er than the moon's sphere,   Swift - er than the moon's

sphere.   The cow-slips tall her pen-sion-ers be; In their gold coats spots you

see; I do wan-der ev - 'ry where, Swift - er than the moon's

sphere;   I do wan-der ev-'ry where,

Swift - er than the moon's— sphere; Swift - er than the moon's—

sphere, Swift - er than— the moon's— sphere;   O-ver hill,   o-ver

dale,   O-ver park,   o-ver pale,   o-ver

hill,   o-ver dale,   Tho-rough bush,   Tho-rough briar,   O-ver park,   o-ver pale,   Tho-rough

pp

flood,   tho-rough fire,   O-ver hill,   o-ver dale,   Tho-rough bush,   tho-rough briar,   O-ver

park,   o-ver pale,   Tho-rough flood,   tho-rough fire,   I do wan -

cresc.

- - - - - - der ev - - 'ry where,

a poco   *ff*   *p*

I do wan-der ev - 'ry where,

Swift- er than the moon's_

sphere;

I do wan-der ev - 'ry where,

Swift - er than the moon's_ sphere;

p dolce

The cow-slips tall her pen-sion-ers

be; In their gold coats spots you see; I do_ wan-der ev - 'ry

cresc.

BID ME DISCOURSE

WILLIAM SHAKSPERE
Sonnet from "Venus and Adonis"

Sir HENRY ROWLEY BISHOP
(1786–1855)

Oliver Ditson Company

M I.—1236–7

Bid me dis-course, I will en - chant thine ear, Or, like a— fair - y

trip up-on the green, I will— en - chant thine— ear,

Or, like— a—— fair - y trip up-on— the— green,

Or, like a— nymph, with bright and flow-ing hair,

seen._____

Bid me dis-course, I will en-chant thine ear, Or, like a fair - y_____

trip up-on__ the__ green, trip, trip, up - on_____ the green,

Bid me dis-course, I will en - chant thine ear,

Or, like a fair-y trip up-on the green,

I will en-chant thine ear, Or, like a fair-y trip up-on the green,

or trip up-on the

Or like a nymph, or like a nymph, with bright and flow-ing hair, with

bright and flow-ing hair, Dance, dance on the sands, dance, dance on the

sands, on the sands, Dance,

cresc. f tr tr
and yet no foot-ing seen, and yet no foot-ing

seen. Dance, Dance, Dance

on the sands, and yet no foot-ing seen, and

yet,_____ and yet no foot-ing seen. Dance,_____

Dance,_____ Dance,_____

_on the sands, and yet no foot-ing seen, and yet,_____ and yet no foot-ing

seen.___

THE WILLOW SONG

WILLIAM SHAKSPERE
From "Othello," Act IV, Scene 3

GIOACHINO ROSSINI
(1792-1868)

all a green_____ wil - low, Sing all a green_____

wil - low; Her salt tears fell from her and sof- ten'd the stones; Sing wil-low,

wil - low, Sing wil - low.

She

sigh'd _____ in ___ her ___ sing - ing, and aft - er each ___

groan; _____ Sing all a green wil - low, Sing all _____ a green

wil - low; I'm dead ___ to all pleas - ure, My true love is gone; O wil-low,

wil-low, O wil - low, O wil - low, wil - low. _____

HARK, HARK! THE LARK

(Composed in 1826)

WILLIAM SHAKSPERE
From "Cymbeline," Act II, Scene 3

(Original Key)

FRANZ SCHUBERT (Posthumous)
(1797-1828)

Hark, hark! the lark at heav'n's gate sings, And Phœbus gins a - rise, ___ His steeds to wa - ter at those springs On cha - lic'd flow'rs that lies; ___ On cha - lic'd flow'rs that lies; And wink - ing Ma - ry-

Oliver Ditson Company

ML.1238-2

WHO IS SYLVIA?

(Composed in 1826)

WILLIAM SHAKSPERE
From "The Two Gentlemen of Verona"
Act IV, Scene 2

(Original Key)

FRANZ SCHUBERT, Op. 106, No. 4
(1797-1828)

ML-1239-2

HARK, HARK! THE LARK

WILLIAM SHAKSPERE
From "Cymbeline," Act II, Scene 3

KARL FRIEDRICH CURSCHMANN
(1805-1841)

Oliver Ditson Company

ML-1240-4

'gins__ a - rise, His steeds__ to wa - ter

at____ those springs On cha - lic'd flow'rs__ that lies;

And wink-ing Ma - ry-buds be - gin To ope their gold - en

eyes: With ev - 'ry thing____ that pret - ty__

bin, _____ My lady sweet, my lady sweet, my

la - dy sweet, a - rise.   A - rise!

A - rise! A - rise!

WHEN THAT I WAS A LITTLE BOY
(CLOWN'S SONG)

WILLIAM SHAKSPERE
Epilogue to "Twelfth Night"

ROBERT SCHUMANN, Op. 127, Nº 5
(1810 - 1856)

When that I was a lit-tle boy, With hey ho, with hey ho, the wind and the rain, A fool-ish thing was but a toy, For the rain, it rain-eth ev-'ry day. But when I came to man's es-tate, With hey ho, with hey ho, the wind and the rain, 'Gainst knaves and thieves men

Oliver Ditson Company

AUTOLYCUS' SONG
(LAWN AS WHITE AS DRIVEN SNOW)

(Original Key, F)

WILLIAM SHAKSPERE
From "A Winter's Tale," Act IV, Scene 4

JAMES GREENHILL
(1840 –)

a) inkles = tapes
b) caddisses = worsted lace

Used in this volume with the kind permission of Messrs Boosey & Co.

cam - brics, and rib - ands of all the col-ours i' the rain - bow!

Allegro vivace

Lawn as white as driv - en snow,

Cy - prus black as e'er was crow; Gloves as sweet as dam-ask ro - ses,

Masks for fa-ces and for no - ses, Masks _____ for fa - ces and for no-ses;

accel.e cresc.

ad lib.

colla voce

Bu - gle, brace-let, neck-lace am-ber,   Per-fume for a la-dy's cham-ber,

Gold-en quoifs and stom-ach-ers,   For my lads to give their dears;

Pins and pok-ing-sticks of steel;[a)]

What maids lack from head to heel.   Come buy of me, come

a) poking-sticks of steel = to stiffen the curls of their ruffs on.

To Sims Reeves

SIGH NO MORE, LADIES

(Original Key)

WILLIAM SHAKSPERE
From "Much Ado About Nothing," Act II, Scene 3

SIR ARTHUR SEYMOUR SULLIVAN
(1842-1900)

Sigh no more, la - dies, sigh no more;

Men were de-ceiv - ers__ ev - - - er; One foot in sea, and

Used in this volume with the kind permission of Messrs Ashdown & Co.

M.L.-1243-4

FEAR NO MORE THE HEAT O' THE SUN

WILLIAM SHAKSPERE
From "Cymbeline," Act IV, Scene 2

(Original Key, G)

Sir C. HUBERT H. PARRY
(1848-   )

M1.-1244-4

Gold - en lads and girls all must, ___ As chim-ney-sweep-ers,

come to dust.

Fear no more the frown o' the great, Thou art

past the ty-rant's stroke; Care no more to clothe and eat; To thee the

122

ML-1244-4

WHO IS SYLVIA?

(Original Key)

WILLIAM SHAKSPERE
From "The Two Gentlemen of Verona," Act IV, Scene 2

MONK GOULD
(1858-   )

Who is Syl - via? what is she, That all— our

swains———————— com - mend her?

ML - 1245 - 5

Ho - - ly,___ fair,___ and

wise___ is___ she;___ The heav'ns___ such grace did

lend her, That she might ad - mir - ed be.

Is___ she kind, as she is

fair?____ For beau-ty lives____ with kind-ness.

Love____ doth____

to____ her eyes____ re - pair,____ To

help____ him of his blind-ness; And be-ing help'd, in-hab-its

there.

Then to Syl - via let us sing, That Syl - via is _____ ex -

cel - ling;

She__ ex - cels__ each mor - tal__ thing,__ Up - on__ the dull earth dwell - ing: To_ her let us gar - lands bring.

BLOW, BLOW, THOU WINTER WIND

WILLIAM SHAKSPERE
From "As You Like It," Act II, Scene 7

(Original Key, C)

WILLIAM ARMS FISHER, Op. 5, No. 4
(1861-   )

Copyright 1897 by Luckhardt & Belder

ML-1246-2

Allegro *poco rit.* *a tempo*

Heigh - ho! sing, heigh - ho! un - to the green hol - ly:___ Heigh - ho! heigh - ho!

Heigh - ho! heigh - ho! Heigh - ho!__ heigh - ho! un - to__ the__ green hol - ly: Most

friend-ship is feign-ing, most lov - ing mere fol - ly: Then, heigh - ho, the hol-ly!

heigh - ho, the hol - ly! This life is most_____ jol - ly.

Jan. 25, 1896

ML-1246-2

SIGH NO MORE, LADIES

(Original Key, F♯ minor)

WILLIAM SHAKSPERE
From "Much Ado About Nothing," Act II, Scene 3

WILLIAM ARMS FISHER, Op. 5, № 5
(1861-)

Copyright 1897 by Luckhardt & Belder

bon - ny, Con - vert - ing all your sounds of woe In - to Hey non - ny, non - ny, non - ny.

Sigh no more, la - dies, sigh no more, la - dies, Be you blithe and

cresc.

bon - ny, be you blithe and bon - ny, Con - vert - ing all your sounds of woe In - to

poco rit.

Hey non - ny, non - ny, non - ny.

a tempo

D. S.

Jan. 31, 1896

ML-1247- 3

To Robert Fulton

IT WAS A LOVER AND HIS LASS

(Original Key, C)

WILLIAM SHAKSPERE
From "As You Like It," Act V, Scene 3

GERARD BARTON
(1861 -)

ML-1248-2

spring-time, the on - ly pret - ty ring - time,

When birds do sing, hey ding-a-ding-a-ding, Sweet lov - ers love the

spring, When birds do sing, hey ding - a - ding - a - ding,_____ Sweet

1. 2. 3.   4.

lov - ers love the spring.___   lov - ers love the spring.___

To Miss Helen Buckley

ORPHEUS WITH HIS LUTE

WILLIAM SHAKSPERE
From "Henry the Eighth," Act III, Scene I

(Original Key)

CARL BUSCH
(1862-   )

ML-1249-3

ORPHEUS WITH HIS LUTE

mu - sic plants and flow'rs Ev - er sprung; as sun and show'rs There had

made a last - ing spring. Ev-'ry thing that heard him play, E'en the

bil - lows of the sea, Hung their heads, and then lay by, Hung their

heads, and then lay by.

To George Hamlin

UNDER THE GREENWOOD TREE

WILLIAM SHAKSPERE
From "As You Like It," Act II, Scene 5

(Original Key)

CARL BUSCH
(1862-   )

ML-1250-3

hith - er, come hith - er, come hith - er: Here shall he see

No en - e - my But win - ter and rough weath - er.

Who doth am - bi - tion shun And

loves to__ live i' the sun, Seek-ing the food he__ eats And pleased with

what he gets,_____ Come hith - er, come hith - er, come

hith - er: Here shall he see_____ No

en - e - my But win - ter and rough weath - er.

AND LET ME THE CANAKIN CLINK
(IAGO'S SONG)

(Original Key)

WILLIAM SHAKSPERE
From "Othello," Act II, Scene 3

HARVEY WORTHINGTON LOOMIS, Op. 10, No 18
(1865-)

CRABBED AGE AND YOUTH

(Original Key, E♭)

WILLIAM SHAKSPERE
From "The Passionate Pilgrim," XII

HARVEY WORTHINGTON LOOMIS, Op. 10, No. 5
(1865-   )

M.L.-1252-3

Youth like sum-mer morn, age like win-ter weath-er; Youth like sum-mer brave, age like

win-ter bare. Youth is full of sport, a-ge's breath is short;

Youth is nim-ble, age is lame; Youth is hot and bold,

age is weak and cold, Youth is wild, and age is tame.

Age, I do ab-hor thee, Youth, I do a-dore thee; O, my love, my

love is young! Age, I do de-fy thee; O sweet shep-herd, hie thee!

For me-thinks thou stay'st too long.

ORPHEUS WITH HIS LUTE

(Original Key, Db)

WILLIAM SHAKSPERE
From "Henry the Eighth," Act III, Scene I

CHARLES FONTEYN MANNEY, Op.3, Nº5
(1872 -   )

ML-1253-3

There had made a last-ing spring, There had made a last-ing

spring.

Ev-'ry thing that heard him play, E'en the bil-lows

of the sea, Hung their heads, and then lay by,

Hung their heads, and then lay by. In sweet mu-sic is such

art,_____ Kill-ing care and grief of heart_____

Fall a-sleep, or hear-ing, die, Fall a-sleep, or hear-ing, die.

IT WAS A LOVER AND HIS LASS

(Original Key)

WILLIAM SHAKSPERE
From "As You Like It," Act V, Scene 3

H. CLOUGH-LEIGHTER
(1874 -   )

M.L.-1254 - 4

O MISTRESS MINE

(Original Key)

WILLIAM SHAKSPERE
From "Twelfth Night," Act II, Scene 3

S. COLERIDGE-TAYLOR
(1875-)

ML - 1255 - 4

What is___ love? 'tis not here-af - ter;

Pres - ent mirth___ hath pres - ent___ laugh - ter; What's to

come___ is still___ un - sure: In de - lay___ there lies___ no